imagine

being deaf

Linda O'Neill

The Rourke Press, Inc.
Vero Beach, Florida 32964

NOTE: Not all of the children photographed in this book are deaf, but volunteered to be
photographed to help raise public awareness.

Thanks to Susan Dolan of Andover, Massachusetts for her assistance in interviewing.

PHOTO CREDITS
© East Coast Studios: cover, pages 6, 13, 17, 18, 24, 29; © Eyewire: page 8;
© Clarke School for the Deaf: page 14

PRODUCED & DESIGNED by East Coast Studios
eastcoaststudios.com

EDITORIAL SERVICES
Pamela Schroeder

Library of Congress Cataloging-in-Publication Data

O'Neill, Linda
   Being deaf / Linda O'Neill.
     p. cm. — (Imagine...)
   Includes index.
   Summary: Defines deafness and its possible causes and describes how deaf people can
communicate through sign language.
   ISBN 1-57103-377-7
   1. Deaf children—Juvenile literature. 2. Deafness—Juvenile literature. [1. Deaf. 2. Physically
handicapped.] I. Title. II. Imagine (Vero Beach, Fla.)

HV2392 .O54 2000
362.4'2'083—dc21

                                                                00–023922

Printed in the USA

Author's Note

This series of books is meant to enlighten and give children an awareness and sensitivity to those people who might not be just like them. We all have obstacles to overcome and challenges to meet. We need to think of the person first, not the disability. The children I interviewed for this series showed not one bit of self-pity. Their spirit and courage is admirable and inspirational.

Linda O'Neill

Table of Contents

Imagine This

Your friend wants to tell you a secret but she can't whisper to you. You can't hear her. You are **deaf** (DEF). You and your friends have to **communicate** (KAH myoo nih KAYT) in a different way. You can write notes. You can use sign language. You can have your own special codes.

Whispering is not the only way to tell secrets.

7

Some people can only hear sounds that are in a certain **pitch** (PICH). Some people cannot hear at all. People who cannot hear at all have **profound** (pro FOWND) hearing loss.

Sometimes no one knows a baby is deaf until he or she is two or three years old. Babies talk at different ages. If a baby doesn't start talking by age two or three, parents become **concerned** (kun SERND).

We learn to talk through many of our senses.

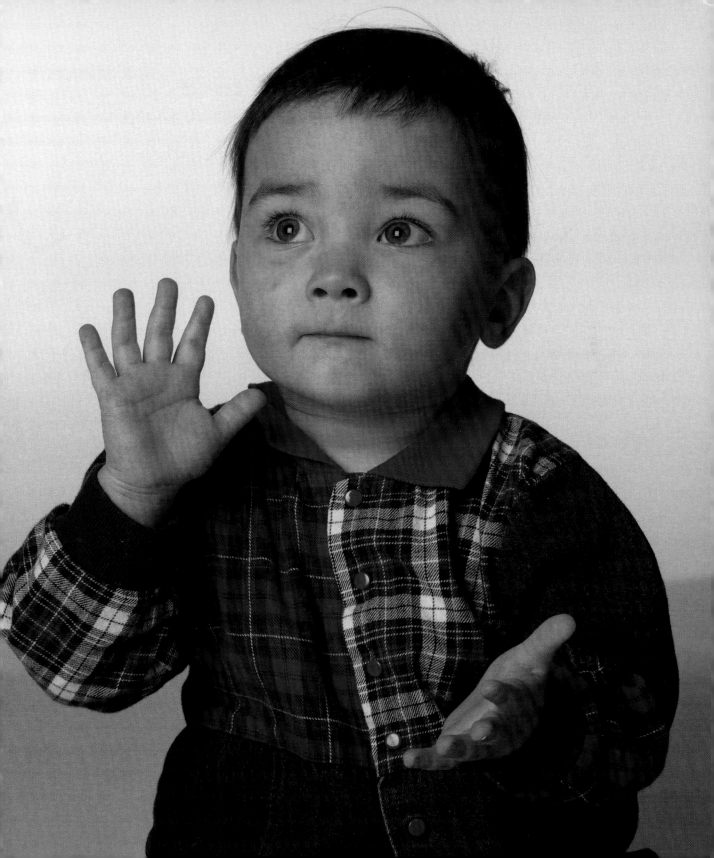

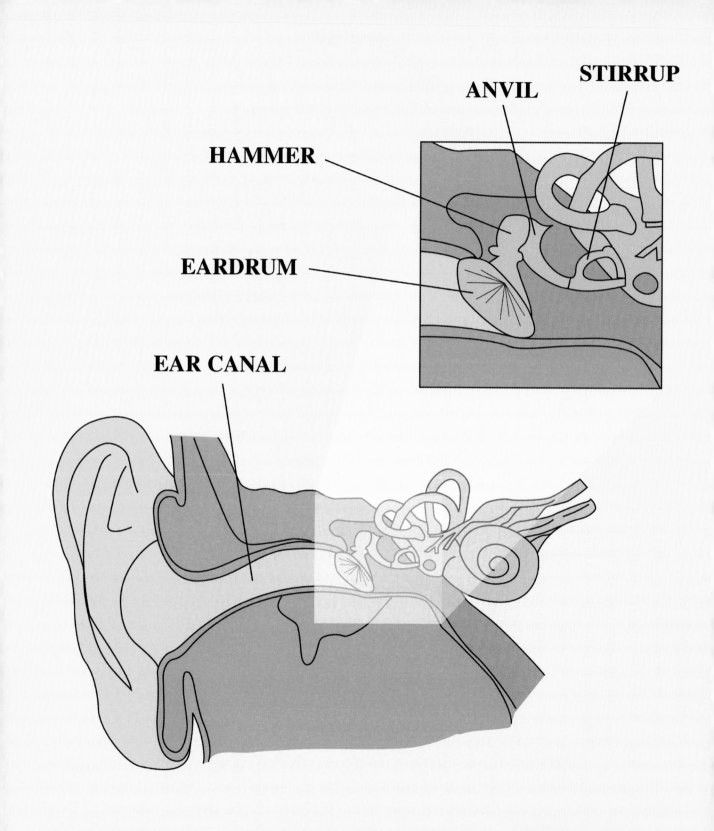

STIRRUP

ANVIL

HAMMER

EARDRUM

EAR CANAL

Causes of Hearing Loss

There are three tiny bones inside our ears that help us hear. They are called the stirrup, the anvil, and the hammer. When they are not working right, we are hearing **impaired** (im PAYRD). Some people are born deaf. Some become deaf when they get hurt or very sick. Loud noises can hurt your hearing, too. You should get a hearing test each year at school to make sure your hearing is O.K.

Three tiny bones inside our ears work together to help us hear.

Speech

When you are a baby, you learn to talk by making the sounds you hear. If you are deaf, you learn to use other **senses** (SEN sez). You watch how your mother's mouth moves when she talks. You feel the breath from her mouth and watch her tongue. Look in the mirror and say these words: "lollipop," "pepper," "fish," bubblegum." Do you see how your mouth moves for each word? Feel the air that comes out of your mouth when you say these words.

A baby watches his mother closely to learn all kinds of things.

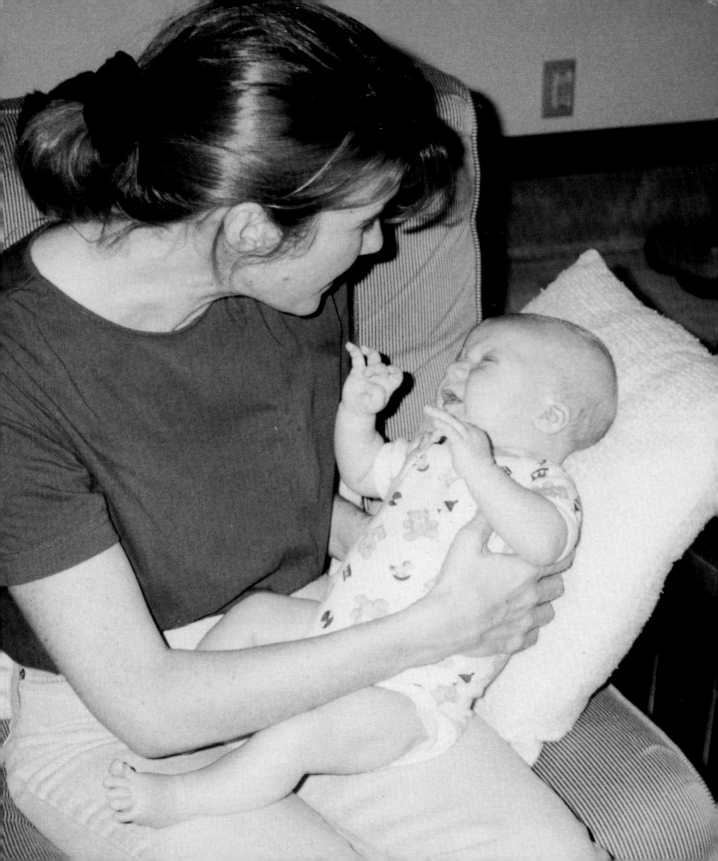

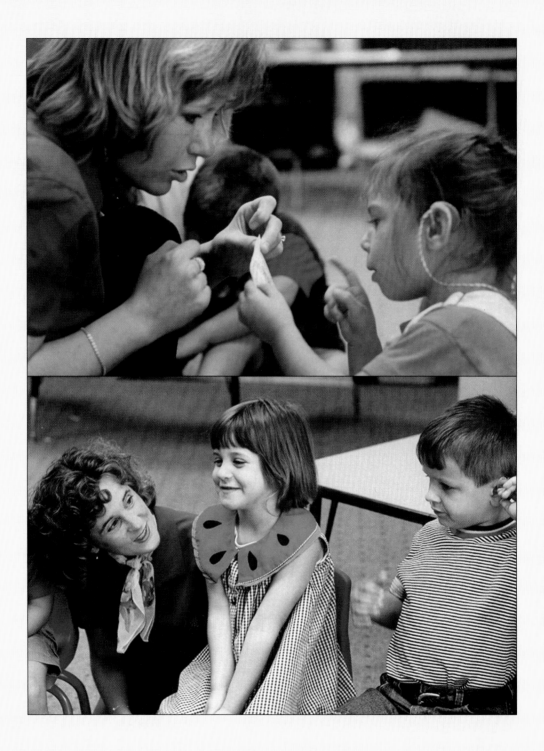

Some children who are born deaf go to special schools to learn to talk. One of the most famous is the Clarke School for the Deaf. It opened in Northampton, Massachusetts, in 1867.

Some children who are deaf go to a school for the hearing impaired.

Speech Reading

Many people who are deaf learn to read lips. This is called speech reading. It takes a lot of practice. Even with practice, a person who is deaf will only get 40 to 50 percent of what you are saying.

When you are talking to hearing impaired people, you should face them so they can see your mouth. By seeing the way your mouth is moving, they can understand the words you are saying.

Looking right at the person you are speaking to is a good idea when you are practicing speech reading.

Hearing Aids

Hearing aids **amplify** (AM pluh FY) sound. That means they make everything louder. It is like turning up the sound on the radio. Hearing aids come in all sizes. You can have a hearing aid the size of a pocket radio that you wear. Some are so small they fit inside your ear. The doctor tells you which kind is best for you.

Another aid for people who are deaf is closed caption television (CCTV). Anyone can use this. Most televisions have a closed caption choice. CCTV prints out the words from TV shows at the bottom of the screen. Some videos also have closed captions.

CCTV helps the hearing impaired watch television.

Sign Language

Laurent Clerc was born in France in 1785. At one year old, he became deaf. He made up sign language as a way to talk. Sign language is a **visual** (VIZH oo al) language. With sign language, people use their hands and faces to talk to each other. Your hands form letters and words.

Clerc came to the United States in 1815. He was the first deaf teacher. In 1817 he helped open the first school for the deaf in the United States. The American School for the Deaf is still open today.

In sign language, each letter has its own sign. Sayings like "I love you" or "thank you" have a sign, too. You can even sing in sign language! You may see someone on TV using sign language next to someone who is talking. He or she is **translating** (TRANZ layt ing) the words into sign language.

It can be fun to learn sign language. You can "talk" without making a sound. If you have friends who are deaf, it is important to be able to communicate with them. Think what it would be like if no one could understand you.

You can take classes to learn sign language. You can learn some sign language on a computer.

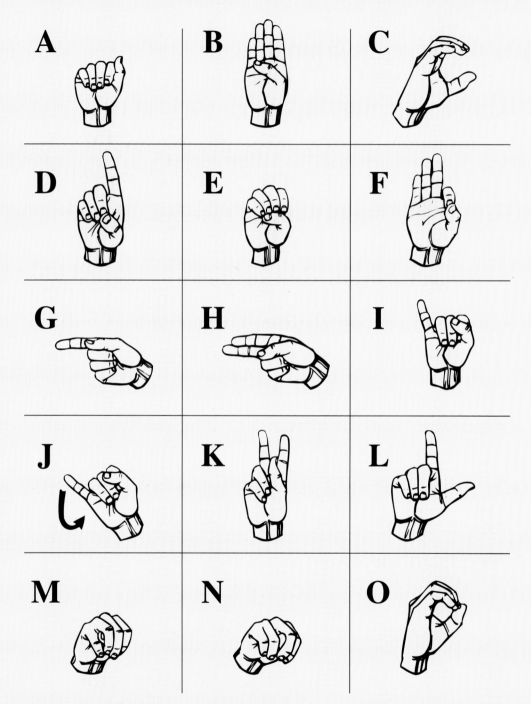

American sign language alphabet.

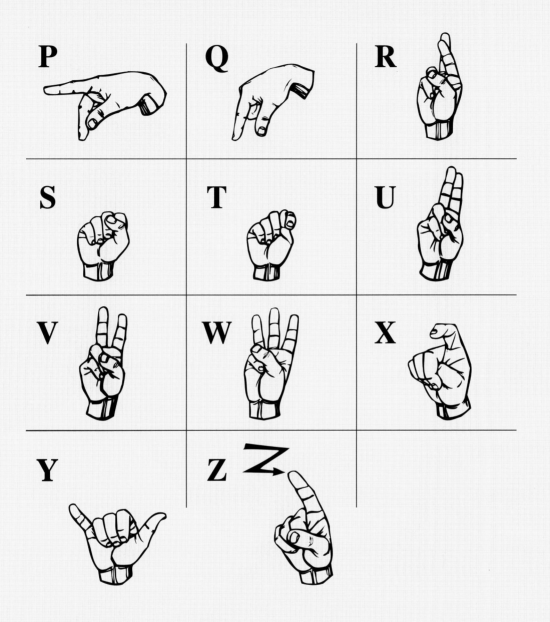

Sign Language We All Use

We use a kind of sign language every day. A shrug means, "who knows?" If we frown, that says we are unhappy. If we put our fingers to our lips, it means "quiet." Think of all the ways we can talk to each other without saying a word. What do you do if you are angry? Do you laugh when you are happy? Do you cry when you are sad? Do you hug your brothers or sisters to let them know you're glad to see them? How many hamburgers do you want? You can hold up one—or two fingers if you are really hungry!

In these ways, we communicate. We all know a smile is a smile in any language.

We all use a kind of sign language.

Meet Someone Special!

Meet Kyle

Kyle, are you deaf or hearing impaired?
   "I'm deaf."

Were you born deaf?
   "Yes."

Do you have brothers and sisters?
   "I have a brother and a sister. They can both hear."

Do they know sign language?
   "My whole family knows sign language. They went to school for it."

Do you read lips?

"A little."

Do you wear hearing aids?

"Sometimes I do but I don't really like them."

What would you like to see made for people who are deaf?

"At the movies there are no words I can see. I can only understand some of the movie. I would like to have a person signing for me so I can know everything being said."

What would you like other kids to know about being hearing impaired?

"I would like other kids not to treat me differently. I want other kids to know we are the same, hearing and deaf. I would like kids to learn sign language. It's hard to go to school with so many hearing kids. I feel lonely. It's hard to understand hearing people. I would like my hearing friends to learn some sign language. Deaf people can do anything hearing people can do. Only we can't hear. It would be good if everyone learned sign language."

What would you like to say to everyone?

"I would like sign language taught in all schools. I wish there were a lot of deaf people. I could have more friends."

Learning sign language can be fun.

Glossary

amplify (AM pluh FY) — to make louder

communicate (KAH myoo nih KAYT) — a way to talk or send messages

concerned (kun SERND) — worried

deaf (DEF) — unable to hear sounds

impaired (im PAYRD) — damaged or hurt, not working right

pitch (PICH) — the tone of sound; high or low

profound (pro FOWND) — complete, total

senses (SEN sez) — how people and animals learn about the world around them: sight, taste, touch, smell, hearing

translate (TRANZ layt) — to change from one language to another

visual (VIZH oo al) — using the sense of sight

Further Reading

James, R. *Ears.* Rourke Press, 1996

Pluckrose, Henry. *Listening and Hearing.* Raintree/Steck Vaughn, 1998

Walpole, Brenda. *Hearing.* Steck-Vaughn Co., 1997

Visit These Websites

dww.deafworldweb.org

www.where.com/scott.net/asl/abc.html

Clarke School for the Deaf
   www.clarkeschool.org

Index